# First Steps Reading Book 2

Gail Porter and Penny Hancock

**Series advisors:**
*Uganda:* Harriet Mutumba, Kindergarten Headmistress and Specialist in Teaching English as a Second Language
*Ghana:* JK Aboagye, Dean, Division of Specialised Professional Studies in Education, University College of Education, Winneba
*Malawi:* Charlotte Day, Lecturer in Early Childhood Development, Care and Education, Chancellor College, University of Malawi
*Kenya:* Ann Njenga, Senior Inspector of Schools, Early Childhood Education, Ministry of Education, Science and Technology
Barbara Koech, Coordinator, Centre for Early Childhood Education, Kenyatta University

## Contents

| | |
|---|---|
| Introduction/Scope and sequence | 2 |

| | | |
|---|---|---|
| **1 Animals** | | **4** |
| Animals at home | | 4 |
| Animal families | | 6 |
| Going to market | | 8 |
| Small wild animals | | 10 |
| Baby animals | | 12 |
| **2 My school** | | **14** |
| My teacher | | 14 |
| Things in the classroom | | 16 |
| My best friend | | 18 |
| The school buildings | | 20 |
| Playtime | | 22 |
| **3 Food** | | **24** |
| My favourite food | | 24 |
| Healthy food | | 26 |
| Growing food | | 28 |
| Food from animals | | 30 |
| Feasts | | 32 |
| **4 Weather and sky** | | **34** |
| Wet and dry | | 34 |
| Shadows and the sun | | 36 |
| The wind | | 38 |
| Day and night | | 40 |
| The sky | | 42 |
| **5 Water and air** | | **44** |
| Uses for water | | 44 |
| Saving water | | 46 |
| Floating and sinking | | 48 |
| Bubbles | | 50 |
| Who lives in water? | | 52 |
| **6 Senses** | | **54** |
| I can see | | 54 |
| I can hear | | 56 |
| I can smell | | 58 |
| I can feel | | 60 |
| I can taste | | 62 |

# Scope and sequence chart: Year Two

| THEME | TOPIC | LANGUAGE | READING SKILLS | WRITING SKILLS | NUMBER SKILLS |
|---|---|---|---|---|---|
| **Term 1: Units 1–10** | | | | | |
| Animals | 1 Animals at home | • domestic animals | • revision of beginning sounds + /a/<br>• rhymes with cat<br>• following picture instructions/story<br>• attention to detail | • drawing from instructions (ant)<br>• copying pictures<br>• letter a | • revision of 1 to 5, value and numeral recognition<br>• categorising<br>• addition of 2; 2 more |
| | 2 Animal families | • male, female and young of familiar animals | • rhymes with ram/hen<br>• following a picture story<br>• beginning sound /e/ | • drawing from picture instructions (hen)<br>• letter e (anti-clockwise spirals → e)<br>• copying pictures | • revision of addition<br>• addition of 3; 3 more<br>• comparing sets to find more |
| | 3 At the market | • transport and produce<br>• preposition: **in** | • revision of beginning sounds<br>• following a picture story<br>• beginning sound /i/<br>• rhymes with chick | • letter i (zigzags → i)<br>• copying pictures | • categorising and reasoning<br>• number sequence; sequencing 1–4<br>• revision of 2 more (up to total of 5)<br>• matching disparate sets<br>• ordinals: first, second, third, last |
| | 4 Small wild animals | • small mammals, birds, reptiles, insects<br>• prepositions: **on, off** | • revision of beginning sounds + /o/<br>• following picture instructions<br>• differentiation including e and c, l and i<br>• rhymes with dog | • drawing from picture instructions<br>• completing pictures<br>• letter o | • revision of ordinals: 1st, 2nd, 3rd, last<br>• revision +3 (up to total of 5)<br>• matching disparate sets<br>• revision of 1–4 value, and shapes |
| | 5 Baby animals | • mothers and babies<br>• prepositions: **under, up** | • following a picture story<br>• rhymes with pup<br>• beginning sound u /ʌ/<br>• following picture instructions | • letter u (∧∧∧∧ → u)<br>• copying pictures<br>• drawing from instructions | • categorising (by relationship)<br>• more; comparing (by size)<br>• ordering 1–3<br>• conservation of number<br>• revision of addition<br>• comparing disparate sets |
| My school | 6 My teacher | • classroom activities | • beginning sound j /dʒ/ | • following complex paths<br>• letter j<br>• copying pictures | • revision of number 4<br>• sets 1–5 and matching numerals<br>• more than (3)<br>• subtraction 2–1; fewer |
| | 7 Things in the classroom | • classroom items<br>• instructions for lotto game<br>• revision: **yellow** | • beginning sound y /j/<br>• differentiation including u and n, j and y | • letter y<br>• copying pictures | • categorising by usage<br>• subtraction 3–1<br>• revision: 1–5<br>• revision: 2–1, –1, → 0<br>• fewer |
| | 8 My best friend | • feelings and friendships<br>• superlative: **tallest**<br>• revision: **green** | • beginning sound /g/ | • pattern making<br>• free drawing<br>• letter g (anti-clockwise spirals → v) | • measuring (tall/short)<br>• ordering (by height)<br>• 3–1, –1, –1, → 0 |
| | 9 School buildings | • school activities; buildings<br>• superlative: **biggest** | • beginning sound /v/<br>• following (6) picture story | • letter v (vvvvv → v) | • 4–1; 4–1, –1, –1, –1, → 0<br>• fewer |
| | 10 Playtime | • games and play activities<br>• revision: **stripes, spots**<br>• revision: ordinals | • beginning sound /z/<br>• following a picture narrative | • letter z | • revision: ordinals: 1st, 2nd, 3rd, last<br>• 5–1, –1, –1, –1, –1, → 0<br>• order (chronological) 1–4 |
| **Term 2: Units 11–20** | | | | | |
| Food | 11 My favourite food | • food, fruit, vegetables<br>• preferences | • beginning sound /f/<br>• following a picture story<br>• visual memory | • free drawing<br>• letter f ( ⌄⌄⌄⌄, ⌐⌐⌐⌐ )<br>• copying pictures | • revision: sets 1–5<br>• revision: subtraction 5–1 → 0 |
| | 12 Healthy food | • advice | • beginning sound /m/<br>• rhymes /iːt/<br>• rhymes -at | • letter m<br>• copying pictures | • categorising<br>• revision: 1–5; more<br>• most<br>• 5–2–1=0 |
| | 13 Growing food | • planting, growing<br>• natural fertilisers | • beginning sound /d/<br>• following picture stories (chronological)<br>• rhymes with hot | • following complex paths<br>• letter d (vvvvv, ℓℓℓℓ )<br>• copying pictures | • revision: 1–5; 2+3=5, 1+4=5<br>• revision: most<br>• revision: tallest/shortest out of 5 items |
| | 14 Food from animals | • animal products | • beginning sound /k/<br>• rhymes with bee<br>• visual memory | • letter k ( vvvvv, //\\// )<br>• copying pictures | • missing; categorising<br>• more/fewer<br>• subtraction: –4 (→ 0); revision: 1–5 |
| | 15 Feasts | • celebrations | • last sound /ks/ x<br>• rhymes with ox<br>• visual memory | • letter x ( vvvvv, //\\// )<br>• copying pictures | • revision: addition<br>• revision: fewer; fewest/most<br>• 1:1; conservation of value |

## Weather and sky

| | Unit | Content | Language | Writing / tracing | Maths |
|---|---|---|---|---|---|
| Weather and sky | 16 Wet and dry | • rainy scene and scenery <br>• activities associated with rainy and dry seasons | • look and say words: **wet, dry** <br>• rhymes with wet <br>• rhymes with dry | • d, r, y → dry <br>• free drawing <br>• wet (tracing) | • time: seasons <br>• 6 – value and numeral <br>• writing numeral 6 |
| | 17 Shadows and the sun | • making shadows | • look and say words: **sun, cat** <br>• matching shapes <br>• rhymes with sun; cat <br>• narrative order; picture story | • s, u, n → sun <br>• cat (tracing) <br>• free drawing | • time of the day <br>• 7: numeral and value <br>• writing numeral 7 <br>• sets 1–7 |
| | 18 Wind | • windy weather <br>• opposites: **wet, dry,** etc. | • following picture instructions <br>• look and say words: **pin, wind** <br>• rhymes with pin | • pin (tracing); w, i, n, d → wind <br>• free drawing <br>• drawing from picture instructions | • 8 – numeral and value <br>• writing numeral 8 <br>• numerical order 1–8 |
| | 19 Day and night | • sky at night and daytime <br>• nocturnal animals <br>• storms | • look and say word: **sky** + rhymes <br>• differentiation: small details and orientation <br>• revision: initial sounds /s/m/ | • free drawing <br>• s, k, y → sky | • 9 – numeral and value |
| | 20 The sky | • revision of colours: red → purple <br>• weather and rainbows | • revision: **sun, wind** <br>• narrative sequence <br>• word and picture matching (rain, sun, wind) | • r, a, i, n → rain <br>• free drawing <br>• colouring in | • ordering (chronological) <br>• 10 – numeral and value <br>• matching numerals and sets 1–10 |

## Term 3: Units 21–30

| | Unit | Content | Language | Writing / tracing | Maths |
|---|---|---|---|---|---|
| Water and air | 21 Uses for water | • activities with water | • look and say words: **cup, tap, jug** <br>• attention to detail <br>• matching shapes, words and pictures | • c, u, p → cup <br>• free drawing | • measuring – volume; most (volume) <br>• addition → 6 <br>• number line 1–10 |
| | 22 Saving water | • containers for water | • look and say words: **pan, tin, lid** <br>• rhymes: pan | • p, a, n → pan | • addition → 7 <br>• number line |
| | 23 Floating and sinking | • things that float <br>• things that sink | • look and say words: **nut, top** <br>• following a picture story/instructions <br>• matching words and pictures | • nut, top, lid, pin (tracing) | • addition → 8; number line sets; ordering <br>• more |
| | 24 Bubbles | • things that dissolve | • following picture instructions <br>• look and say words: **soap, bar, ink, oil** <br>• rhymes with bar <br>• words and picture matching <br>• differentiation (small detail) | • b, a, r → bar <br>• ink, oil (tracing) | • subtraction: 6 minus (1–6) <br>• number sequence (1–10) <br>• one (less) |
| | 25 Who lives in water? | • story of Noah's ark <br>• underwater and water creatures | • look and say words: **ark, duck, fish, frog** <br>• narrative sequence <br>• matching same patterns | • a, r, k → ark <br>• frog, fish, duck (tracing) <br>• free drawing | • addition → 9 <br>• number line <br>• categorising |
| Senses | 26 I can see | • seeing; eyes <br>• creatures, especially insects | • beginning sounds including /m/ <br>• following picture instructions for a game <br>• phonics: an + c, d, p, m, t; rhymes: -an <br>• look and say: **I can see** | • I can see a … (tracing) | • addition → 10 |
| | 27 I can hear | • sounds, volume | • following picture game/instructions <br>• phonics: in + t, p, b <br>• look and say word: **hear** <br>• matching pictures and short sentences | • t, i, n → tin <br>• **I can hear a …in** <br>• **pin in a tin/tin in a bin** (tracing) | • subtraction from 7 <br>• number sequence (1–10) <br>• sets <br>• conservation |
| | 28 I can smell | • smells, likes and dislikes | • following a picture narrative and sequencing <br>• look and say word: **smell, fire** <br>• phonics: at + c, m, h <br>• matching pictures and short sentences | • h, a, t → hat <br>• **cat in a hat/cat on a mat** (tracing) | • subtraction from 8 <br>• sets of 8 <br>• pattern making |
| | 29 I can feel | • touch: texture and sensations | • following a picture story <br>• rhymes with hot <br>• look and say words: **is the** <br>• narrative sequence; short sentences | • p, o, t → pot <br>• **The cat is hot/The cat is not hot** (tracing) | • subtraction from 9 <br>• categorising <br>• revision: 1–9, numerals and value |
| | 30 I can taste | • taste, food | • following picture instructions to play a game; following a picture narrative word and picture matching <br>• rhymes with nut <br>• look and say words: **taste, bad, good, It** <br>• phonics: n, h + ut and b, f + ox <br>• short sentences | • n, u, t → nut <br>• **I can taste a …** <br>• The (fox) is (in) the box | • subtraction from 10 <br>• revision 1–10 |

# 1 Animals

## Animals at home

Ask: *What can you see?* Talk about the picture. Ask: *Is your home like this?* Say: *Name the animals.* Ask: *What is the beginning sound in 'animal'? What is the beginning sound in each animal?*

Say: *Look at the pictures.* Ask: *What is happening in each picture?* Help the children to tell the story from the pictures. Ask: *What do you think will happen next? What is the beginning sound in 'ant'? What other things begin with the sound 'a'?*

Week 1 *Animals at home* 5

# Animal families

chickens

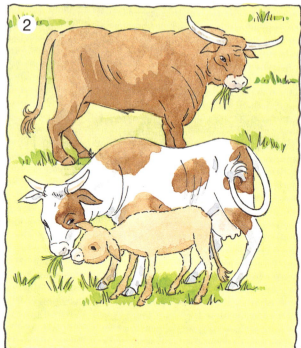

cattle

goats

sheep

Say: *Look at the pictures*. Talk about animal families. Ask: *Do you have these animals at home? Which two animals rhyme?*

6 Week 2 *Animal families*

# The hen and the egg

Say: *Tell the story from the pictures.* Ask: *What is the beginning sound in 'egg'?*

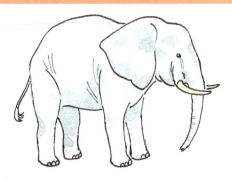
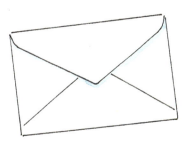

Say: *Name these pictures to find other words beginning with the sound 'e'.*

Week 2 *Animal families*

# Going to market

Ask: *What is happening? Have you been to a market like this?* Say: *Name the animals.* Ask: *What is the beginning sound in the words?*

Week 3 *Going to market*

# The lazy donkey

Say: *Tell the story from the pictures.* Ask: *What is the beginning sound in 'insect'?*

Say: *Name the pictures to find other words beginning with the sound 'i'.*

Week 3 *Going to market*

# Small wild animals

Ask: *What can you see?* Say: *Name the animals.* Ask: *What animals do you have near your home?* Say: *Draw them.*

10  Week 4 *Small wild animals*

Say: Tell the story from the pictures. Ask: What is the frog doing in each picture? What is the beginning sound in 'on'? What other things begin with the sound 'o'?

Week 4 *Small wild animals*

# Baby animals

Ask: *What can you see in the pictures?* Say: *Name the baby animals and their mothers.*

# Where is his mum?

Say: *Tell the story from the pictures.*

Say: *Tell the story from the pictures.* Ask: *Where is the kitten? What is the beginning sound in 'up'? What other things begin with the sound 'u'?*

Week 5 *Baby animals* 13

# 2 My school

## My teacher

Talk with the children about the teacher. Ask: *Who is this? Where is the number 4?* Say: *Find a jar.* Ask: *What other things begin with the sound 'j'?*

Ask: *What is the teacher doing in each picture? Which things do you like doing at school?*

Week 6 *My teacher*

# Things in the classroom

Say: *Name the things in the frame. Find the things hidden in the picture.* Ask: *What is yellow? What vegetable begins with the sound 'y' as in 'yellow'?*

Ask: *What is she saying? What is the beginning sound?*

Say: *Cover any two pictures with bottle tops. Listen to me. Cover the things I name with more bottle tops. When all your pictures are covered, put up your hand.*

Week 7 *Things in the classroom*

# My best friend

Ask: *What has happened?* Say: *Tell the story.* Ask: *Who is helping? Who is not? How do they feel? What animal can you see? What is the beginning sound in 'goat'? What other things begin with the sound 'g'?*

Week 8 *My best friend*

Say: Talk about friends. Ask: What things do friends do together? What things begin with the sound 'g'? Who is tall? Who is short?

Week 8 *My best friend*

# The school buildings

Ask: *Where are the children going? What have they been doing?* Say: *Name the different parts of the school.* Ask: *What do you do in each place? What is standing outside the school? What is the beginning sound? What other things begin with the sound 'v' as in 'van'?*

Say: Tell the story from the pictures. Ask: What things begin with 'v' as in 'van'?

Week 9 *The school buildings*

# Playtime

Ask: *What are they doing? Do you do these things in playtime? What is the beginning sound in 'zigzag'? What other things begin with the sound 'z'?*

Ask: *What are the children playing? Do you know? Who is first? What is the second child wearing? What is the last child wearing?* Say: *Play the game 'Follow the leader'.*

Week 10 *Playtime*

# 3 Food

## My favourite food

Ask: *What is their favourite food? What is your favourite food? What is the first sound in 'food'? What other things begin with the sound 'f'?*

Week 11 *My favourite food*

Say: Tell the story from the pictures. Ask: How many things did they buy? What did they buy? What things begin with 'f' as in 'fat'? What things rhyme with 'fat'?

Week 11 *My favourite food*

# Healthy food

Ask: *What are these foods good for? What is the first sound in 'milk'? What other things begin with the sound 'm'?*

Ask: *What food is bad for your teeth and body? What pair of things rhymes with 'sweet'?*

Week 12 *Healthy food* **27**

# Growing food

Ask: *What things do plants need to grow and make food? What are the children doing? What is the first sound in 'digging'? What other things begin with the sound 'd'?*

28  Week 13 *Growing food*

a

b

Say: *Tell the stories from the pictures.* Ask: *Why does the plant in story a grow? What happens to the plant in story b? Why?* Say: *Find two things that rhyme with 'hot'.*

Week 13 *Growing food* 29

# Food from animals

Ask: *What food can you see in the picture? Where does it come from? Where is it cooked? What is the first sound in 'kitchen'? What other things begin with the sound 'k'?*

Say: *Name the food.* Talk with the children about how we get food from animals and plants. Ask: *What rhymes with 'bee'?*

Week 14 *Food from animals*

# Feasts

Ask: *What is everybody doing? What do you think is going to happen? What rhymes with 'ox'? What is the last sound?*

Ask: *What are these people celebrating? Have you been to a feast?* Talk with the children about what happens.

Week 15 *Feasts* 33

# 4 Weather and sky

**Wet and dry**

dry

Talk with the children about the picture. Ask: *What is happening? What season is it? What rhymes with 'dry'?*

wet

Talk with the children about the picture. Ask: *What is happening? What season is it?*

# Shadows and the sun

Ask: *What is the sun doing? What time of day is it in each picture? What is happening to the shadow? Have you got a shadow? Have you got a shadow all the time?*

sun

36   Week 17 *Shadows and the sun*

# The scary monster

Say: *Tell the story.* Ask: *How does she feel?*

cat

# The wind

Say: *Make a windmill. Use your windmill outside.* Ask: *Is there any wind? Where is it coming from?*

pin

# The wind story

Talk about the picture with the children. Ask: *What is happening?*

wind

Week 18 *The wind* 39

# Day and night

Ask: *Can you see these things in the sky?* Say: *Take a look. Say what you can see.*

Ask: *What can you see in the sky at night?*

sky

Ask: *Have you seen a thunderstorm? What does it sound like? What does it look like? What colour can you see in the picture?* Say: *Draw a thunderstorm.*

Week 19 *Day and night*

# The sky

Say: Tell the story from the pictures. Ask: What colours can you see? What is grey? Have you ever seen a rainbow?

rain

**42** Week 20 *The sky*

Ask: *What is the weather like in each picture? What is the weather like today? What does the sky look like in each picture? What does the sky look like today? Which weather do you like best?* Say: *Draw it.*

Week 20 *The sky*

# 5 Water and air

## Uses for water

Say: *Talk about the pictures.* Ask: *What do you do with water?* Say: *Name other things you use water for.*

cup

Ask: *What shape are the cups? Which cup has more orange juice?* Say: *Play this game with different shaped cups.*

cup    tap    jug

Week 21 *Uses for water*

# Saving water

Say: Tell the story from the pictures. Ask: Why did the farmer put buckets out?

tin      pan

46 Week 22 *Saving water*

Ask: *How can you save water?*

tap

lid

Week 22 *Saving water*

# Floating and sinking

Ask: *What floats? What sinks?* Say: *Play this game yourself. Try different things.*

nut    top

# The crow and the jug

Say: *Tell the story from the pictures.* Ask: *Did the crow put more water in?* Say: *Try this yourself.*

Week 23 *Floating and sinking*

# Bubbles

Say: Tell the story from the pictures. Make bubbles yourself. Ask: What is inside the bubbles?

 bar of soap

Ask: *What things dissolve in water?* Say: *Try different things yourself.*

Week 24 *Bubbles*

# Who lives in water?

Say: Tell the story from the pictures. Ask: Why did the animals go into the ark? Who did not go into the ark? Why?

ark

Say: *Name these creatures.* Ask: *Which ones live under water?*

fish                          frog                                duck

Week 25 *Who lives in water?* **53**

# 6 Senses

I can see

Ask: Which eyes are like yours? What can these eyes see? What are the first sounds?

I       can       see

Say: Tell the story from the pictures. Play the game yourself.

an      can      man      ant      and

Week 26 *I can see* 55

# I can hear

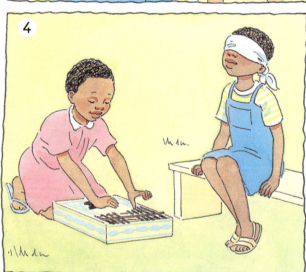

Ask: *What can she hear?* Say: *Play this game with me.*

in                    bin                    tin

# How to make a rattle

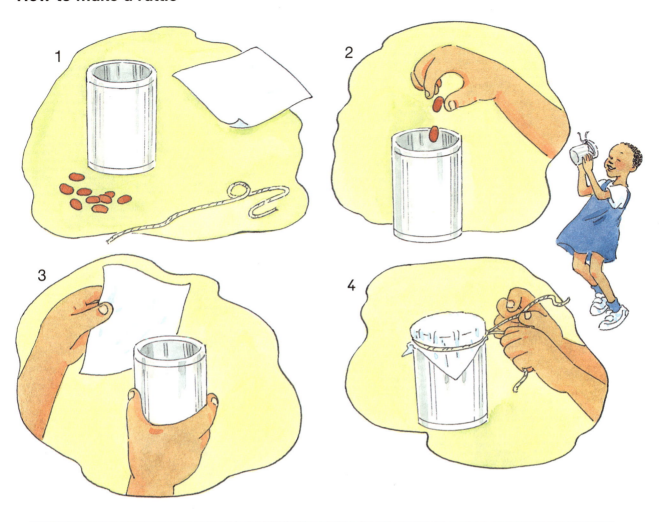

Say: *Make a rattle. Make a loud sound. Make a soft sound. Try different materials inside the rattle.*

pin in a tin

Week 27 *I can hear* 57

# I can smell

Say: *Smell things in our classroom.* Ask: *What smells good? What smells bad? Which smells do the children in the pictures like?*

at      cat      hat      mat

Say: Tell the story from the pictures. Ask: Why is smell useful?

Week 28 I can smell

# I can feel

The mat feels wet.

The hat feels dry.

The pot feels hot.

The pot is not hot.

Say: *Talk about the pictures.* Ask: *Can you read the words?* Say: *Touch things in the classroom.* Ask: *How do they feel?*

the          feel          is

The cat is hot.

The cat is not hot.

The cat is wet.

The cat is not wet.

Say: Tell the story from the pictures. Ask: Can you read the words? How does the cat feel in each picture? Which feelings do you like?

ot　　　hot　　　not　　　pot

# I can taste

Ask: *What is happening in the picture?* Say: *Play this game yourselves.* Ask: *Which tastes do you like? Which tastes don't you like?*

 nut

 jug

The fox is in the box.
The ox is not in the box.

Say: Tell the story from the pictures. Ask: What is the fox tasting? What does each food taste like to the fox? Which food does the fox like? What do you think each food tastes like?

Week 30 *I can taste* 63

© Copyright text Gail Porter and Penny Hancock, 2001
© Copyright illustrations Macmillan Education Ltd, 2001

All rights reserved. No reproduction, copy or transmission of this publication may be made without written permission.

No paragraph of this publication may be reproduced, copied or transmitted save with written permission or in accordance with the provisions of the Copyright, Designs and Patents Act 1988, or under the terms of any licence permitting limited copying issued by the Copyright Licensing Agency, 90 Tottenham Court Road, London W1P 9HE.

Any person who does any unauthorised act in relation to this publication may be liable to criminal prosecution and civil claims for damages.

First published in 2001 by
MACMILLAN EDUCATION LTD
London and Oxford
*Companies and representatives throughout the world*
www.macmillan-africa.com

ISBN 0-333-74054-8

| 10 | 9  | 8  | 7  | 6  | 5  | 4  | 3  | 2  | 1  |
|----|----|----|----|----|----|----|----|----|----|
| 10 | 09 | 08 | 07 | 06 | 05 | 04 | 03 | 02 | 01 |

This book is printed on paper suitable for recycling and made from fully managed and sustained forest sources.

Typeset by Dave Glover

Printed in Malaysia

A catalogue record for this book is available from the British Library

Illustrations by Liz MacIntosh and Lynda Knott
Cover design by Stafford and Stafford
Cover illustration by Liz MacIntosh